The Life of Plants

Plant Habitats

Richard & Louise Spilsbury

Heinemann
LIBRARY

www.heinemann.co.uk
Visit our website to find out more information about **Heinemann Library** books.

To order:
 Phone 44 (0) 1865 888066
Send a fax to 44 (0) 1865 314091
Visit the Heinemann Bookshop at www.heinemann.co.uk to browse our catalogue and order online.

First published in Great Britain by Heinemann Library,
Halley Court, Jordan Hill, Oxford OX2 8EJ
a division of Harcourt Education
Heinemann is a registered trademark of Harcourt Education Ltd.

Designed by Macwiz
Illustrated by Jeff Edwards
Originated by Ambassador Litho Ltd
Printed by Wing King Tong, Hong Kong

ISBN 0 431 11884 1 (hardback)
06 05 04 03 02
10 9 8 7 6 5 4 3 2 1

British Library Cataloguing in Publication Data

Spilsbury, Louise
    Plant habitat. - (Life of plants)
    1. Plant physiology - Juvenile literature
    I. Title II. Spilsbury, Richard, 1963-
    581.7

Acknowledgements

The Publishers would like to thank the following for permission to reproduce photographs: Corbis: pp7, 13, 16, 17, 23, 27, 29, 30, 31, 37, 38, 39; FLPA: pp8, 18; Holt Studios: pp4, 9, 11, 14, 20, 21, 22, 24, 26, 34, 35, 36; Oxford Scientific Films: pp6, 10, 12, 15, 19, 25, 32, 33, 28; Hemera: cone motif

Cover photograph reproduced with permission of Corbis

Our thanks to Andrew Solway for his comments in the preparation of this book.

Every effort has been made to contact copyright holders of any material reproduced in this book. Any omissions will be rectified in subsequent printings if notice is given to the Publisher.

Contents

Any words appearing in the text in bold, **like this**, are explained in the glossary.

A plant may be called different things in different countries, so every type of plant has a Latin name that can be recognized anywhere in the world. Latin names are made of two words – the first is the genus (general group) a plant belongs to and the second is its species (specific) name. Latin plant names are given in brackets throughout this book.

A world of plants

You can find plants growing just about anywhere in the world – from burning hot deserts to the icy lands near the **Poles**, and from wind-blasted mountaintops to the lonely heart of the oceans. The kind of place in which a plant usually lives in nature is called its **habitat** and different kinds of plants grow in different habitats.

Adapt to survive

People can live in all sorts of habitats. When we visit a different place we can **adapt** by taking what we need with us – extra water and sunhats for hot deserts, warm clothes and hot drinks for icy lands. Unlike us, plants cannot move around. They live in one place for their whole lives and have to grow in ways that are ideally suited to their particular habitat. Some plants, such as the cactus, have special features that enable them to live in hot, dry deserts. Others, like water lilies, grow in ways that ensure they can survive in the ponds and lakes where they live.

Over thousands of years, plants gradually adapt to their habitat – they begin to grow in ways and forms that make them better able to survive and **reproduce** in the conditions there. This is called adaptation. In this book we look at the different ways plants are adapted to life in the many different habitats found on Earth.

◄ Each habitat of the world is home to a characteristic group of plants. Palm trees like these usually grow in **tropical** places, where it is warm and wet so trees can grow very tall.

Plant habitats of the world

There are many factors that help make the habitats on Earth different from each other. The most obvious is the **climate** – the kind of weather an area has for most of the time. Lands around the **Equator**, an imaginary line around the centre of the Earth, are the hottest places. Lands further away from the Equator, nearer the Poles, are colder. In some places, the weather stays much the same all year round; in others, weather patterns change throughout the year, according to the seasons. Plants are also affected by the amount of rainfall an area has, what the ground is like – for example, whether it is sandy or rocky – and whether the area is sheltered, as in a valley, or exposed to high winds, as on a mountaintop.

▼ This map shows you where some of the different plant habitats of the world are to be found. Note that these habitats are not the same all over. The characteristics of places within a particular habitat will vary, sometimes a little, sometimes a lot.

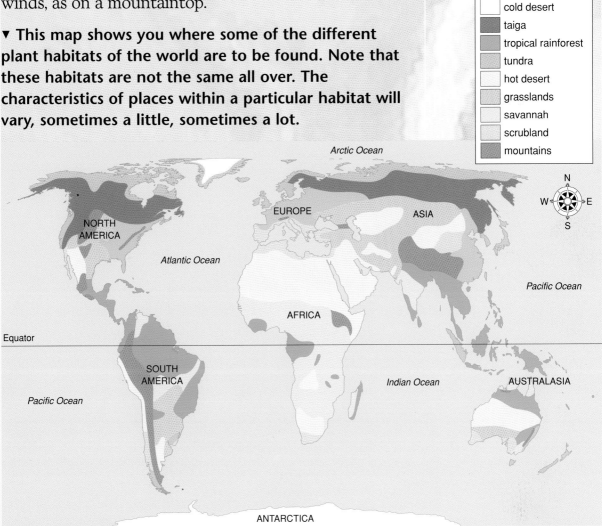

key
- temperate forest
- cold desert
- taiga
- tropical rainforest
- tundra
- hot desert
- grasslands
- savannah
- scrubland
- mountains

Temperate forests

Around 5000 years ago, almost two-thirds of the world's land was covered in forests. Since then, people have cut down more than half the forests to make way for farms and cities. The woodlands that remain form very rich and important **habitats**.

Temperate evergreen forests

Many trees in temperate areas hold on to their leaves during cold seasons. Some temperate forests in the USA are home to giant **conifer** trees, such as redwood (*Sequoia*). Some temperate **evergreen** forests in China are dominated by tree-like plants, such as bamboo (*Phyllostachys*).

Most natural woodland is a mixture of different kinds of trees, but in **temperate** areas, more **broad-leaved** trees, such as maple (*Acer*), oak (*Quercus*) and beech (*Fagus*), grow. Temperate areas have seasons (spring, summer, autumn and winter), and the lifecycles of the trees follow a seasonal pattern. Many broad-leaved trees are **deciduous** – they shed all their leaves in winter because chill winds would damage or destroy them. In spring, fresh leaves form. The trees use their leaves for **photosynthesis** (to make their own food) to give them the **energy** they need for growth and to make flowers, **seeds** and **nuts**.

► Deciduous trees survive the cold winters rather as hibernating animals do – by storing energy in their bodies and resting until spring.

Woodland life

By autumn, trees in a deciduous forest have produced masses of leaves, flowers, seeds and nuts. Woodland creatures, such as squirrels, birds and insects, eat many of these plant parts but others fall to the ground. As this carpet of plant matter – called **leaf litter** – decays, it returns the **nutrients** in the plant parts to the tree's own **roots**, as well as providing nutrients for other plants.

On the forest floor, flowering plants, ferns and **mosses** grow. Ferns and mosses thrive in shady, damp patches, but most flowering plants need plenty of light to grow and **reproduce**. They **germinate** and flower in spring, before the leaves on trees are fully open. At this time of year the forest floor is much lighter. The flowering plants make and spread seeds quickly and new plants grow from these seeds in the following spring. **Perennial** flowering plants, such as bluebells (*Scilla*), sit out the dark times of the year by storing energy in underground **bulbs** or roots, waiting to flower again the following spring.

▲ In forests, mosses and **liverworts** often grow on the trunks of trees in damper places. Shorter trees and **shrubs** grow below the tall trees in spaces where light gets through the **canopy** (roof of leaves).

7

Taiga

Taiga is the name given to forests in northerly parts of the world, where it is very cold in winter and summers are short. Taiga forests mostly contain **conifers**, trees that carry their **seeds** in **cones**, such as pine and fir. How do conifers survive in places where few other trees can and where temperatures are freezing for half the year?

The main reason for the conifers' success is the needle-like shape of their leaves. All leaves contain water and all trees lose some water from their leaves. The water **evaporates** – turns to **water vapour** (a kind of gas) and becomes part of the air. In winter, water in the ground is frozen into ice and plants cannot use it, so it is vitally important for a plant to hold on to any water it has. Needle leaves lose less water than other kinds of leaves. Because they are very thin, there is less space from which the water can escape. The needles are also covered with a thin layer of **wax** that acts like a coat, protecting them from cold and helping to prevent them from drying out.

◄ **Most conifers have branches that angle downwards, giving them a pyramid shape. Instead of gathering on the branches and breaking them, winter snow simply slides off.**

Ever green?

Conifers are often called **evergreens**, because they keep their leaves all year round. They do lose old leaves, a few at a time throughout the year, but they do not drop all their leaves at once as **deciduous** trees do. Keeping their leaves throughout the year gives conifers another advantage. They are able to use their leaves for **photosynthesis** as soon as the summer sun arrives. The warm season is short for most conifers and this is when the trees do most of their growing. Having leaves already means they don't waste precious time growing new ones.

On the forest floor

It is darker on the ground in a **coniferous** forest than in a deciduous one. There is less space between the trees and without winter leaf fall, the light is blocked by leafy branches all year round. Also the ground is less **fertile**. When conifer needles fall, they take longer to rot down than the broad leaves of deciduous trees and the **leaf litter** they form is not so good for other plants to grow in. As a result of lower light levels and poor soil, there is less undergrowth in a coniferous forest than in a deciduous one.

▲ Dark colours absorb heat – you may have noticed this when wearing a dark T-shirt in summer. The dark green colour of conifer needles helps them absorb more heat from the short hours of sunshine in the taiga.

Tropical rainforests

Tropical rainforests lie close to the **Equator**, in an area called the tropics. In this **habitat** there are no seasons; it is warm and sunny and it rains almost every day. Plants have plentiful supplies of everything they need – warmth, sunlight, water and air – making the rainforest the most lush and **fertile** habitat on Earth.

Plants can grow faster here than anywhere else in the world. Rainforest trees such as teak (*Tectona grandis*), mahogany (*Swietenia Macrophylla*) and rosewood (*Aniba rosaeodora*) grow 40 to 50 metres tall. Their leafy branches form a thick green **canopy**, which catches most of the sunlight that falls on the rainforest. **Shrubs** and smaller trees below, such as palms, often have giant leaves to make sure they catch as much of the light that comes through as possible.

▲ Rainforest soil is often shallow and most **nutrients** are only found near the surface, so plants living there have shallow root systems. Tall rainforest trees have wide above-ground buttress roots, which flare at the base to help prop them up.

Rainforest thieves

On the rainforest floor it is often too dark for any but **parasite plants**, such as the giant rafflesia (*Rafflesia arnoldii*), to survive. Parasite plants force their roots into the parts of other plants and steal their water and nutrients.

Up to the light

Some rainforest plants have other ways of getting to the light. Lianas have **roots** in the ground, but as they grow they wrap their **stems** around tree trunks to climb upwards. When they reach the light at the top, they grow colourful flowers.

Others take a short cut. **Epiphytes** are plants that grow high on rainforest branches or trunks. Many orchids and ferns grow like this. Their **seeds** often **germinate** in pockets of rotting plant matter, such as dead **mosses**. They get water from rain and moisture in the air. Many dangle their roots in the air to collect moisture. **Bromeliads** are epiphytes that collect rainwater in **waxy** leaves that form cups. Some hold large pools of water that provide homes for some rainforest creatures, including frogs and salamanders. Animals that die in bromeliad pools decompose (rot away) and provide the plant with nutrients.

◄ Epiphytes are often called air plants, because they are not attached to the ground.

Strangler fig

When a forest animal eats a strangler fig (*Ficus aurea*) fruit, it drops the seeds in the treetops. When the seed germinates, it sends roots all the way down to the forest floor to collect water and nutrients. These many roots thicken and form a cage around the tree, taking its light. Eventually the tree dies, leaving the fully grown strangler fig with a hollow centre.

Tundra

One-fifth of the Earth's surface is covered in frozen land called tundra. Alpine tundra is found at the top of tall, cold mountains and Arctic tundra around the North **Pole**. It hardly ever rains in tundra **habitats**, and water in the ground is locked in ice for most of the year. Most tundra plants only come to life in summer, when the ground thaws for a short time. Even then, plants have to cope with very cold temperatures and strong, icy winds.

Huddle up

When we are blasted by cold winds, our natural inclination is to huddle up and make ourselves smaller. Some plants, such as **moss**, cope with cold in a similar way. They grow in compact forms, like cushions or mats, very close to the ground. By doing this they create a little domed world that traps warmth and moisture inside itself.

Stay low

Other plants grow close to the ground, out of the path of icy winds, in different forms. Many of the plants that grow in extremely cold places look very different from relatives that live in warmer habitats. Most willow trees grow tall with leafy branches. Arctic willows (*Salix polaris*) never grow taller than about 8 or 10 centimetres.

▶ Instead of growing up, the Arctic willow grows across the ground and can be as long as other willow trees are tall!

Goosebumps!

When we are cold, the hairs on our arms and legs stand up to trap a layer of warm air around us (goosebumps). Some plants have fine, hair-like strands on their leaves and **stems** that help to trap warmth in the same way. The edelweiss (*Leontopodium alpina*), a small flowering plant that grows high in the mountains of the Alps, has a layer of woolly hair covering its leaves and flowers.

Underground shelters

Many plants survive the coldest times by resting beneath the ground. Above-ground parts die back at the end of summer and the plant stores **energy** in swollen **roots** or **stems** underground, ready to grow again in the next spring. Some plants live only for the few weeks of warmth, but make **seeds** before they die that survive under the ground, sometimes for many years, until it is warm enough for them to **germinate**.

The flower that melts snow!

The flower **buds** of the alpine snowbell (*Soldanella alpina*) form the year before they flower. The buds survive winter under a blanket of snow. In spring the dark buds absorb sunlight reaching them through the snow, and as the buds warm up they help to melt the snow around them. The snowbells appear as bright patches of colour in the snow.

Deserts

The hot deserts of the world are places of extremes – warm as an oven in the daytime, and often very cold at night; dry for long stretches of time, then suddenly watered by brief rainstorms. How do plants, which need water to live, survive in hot, dry deserts – **habitats** so harsh they are given names like 'Death Valley'?

▲ Saguaro cacti (*Carnegiea gigantea*) grow in deserts in south-western USA and Mexico. They can grow up to 20 m tall (as high as a four-storey house) and live for 200 years.

Collecting water

As rain falls only in short bursts, it is important for plants to collect as much of it as they can. Many plants, such as most cacti, have **roots** that grow just below the surface, but they spread far and wide, ready to collect any dew or rainwater that seeps in. Others, such as the gourd and the saguaro, have very long roots that can reach water sources deep underground.

Desert plants are usually widely spaced out, so their roots do not have to compete with each other for any moisture in the soil. In the American desert the creosote bush (*Larrea tridentata*) grows a dense mat of roots metres wide, to ensure no other plants can grow near it.

Strange but true

The welwitschia plant (*Welwitschia mirabilis*) of the Namib Desert lives for centuries, but grows very, very slowly. It produces only two twisted, leathery leaves. These grow to about 2 metres long, to catch moisture from morning fogs and channel it into the ground, where it is collected by the plant's huge root.

Storing water

Many desert plants, such as cacti, survive by storing water in **succulent** (fleshy) **stems**. Many have pleated or grooved stems, which expand as they fill with water after rain. Cacti shrink again in size as the water is gradually used up.

Some desert plants, such as cacti and euphorbias, use their stems for **photosynthesis** instead of their leaves. Their large stems are green because they contain the **chlorophyll**. Their leaves are shaped like spikes or thorns and they are often brown. With a smaller surface area, these leaves lose less water than flatter ones.

Taking cover

Many desert plants are **annuals**. After a burst of rain, they **germinate**, grow, flower and produce **seeds** in a short time. The seeds they release before they die have a thick seed coat so they can survive underground for a long time, waiting for the next heavy rainfall to start the cycle again. Many smaller **perennials**, plants that live for many years, survive the hottest, driest times underground as **bulbs** and **corms**.

Living stones

Desert plants that store moisture are always at risk from animals in search of a drink, but pebble plants (*Lithops*), which grow in the deserts of Namibia and South Africa, are hardly ever eaten. Their small, fat leaves, swollen with liquid, look just like the stones among which they grow. You can tell they are plants only when they flower!

Grasslands

Across the world there are areas of land where the soil is too poor or the weather too dry for trees and many other plants to grow. Instead grasses take over, covering the land like a vast, living blanket.

The American Prairies

In the USA, areas of grassland are known as prairies. Farmers have ploughed up most of the wild grasses to grow different kinds of grass – cereals such as wheat and corn. Some patches of wild prairie still remain. Different kinds of grass grow in different areas, from tall grass and even patches of trees in the more **humid** areas, to shorter grasses in drier parts. In spring these wild areas are covered in colourful wild flowers, such as pea plants.

▶ Tumbleweed (*Salsola kali*) is a plant found on both prairie and steppe. When it is mature, the plant breaks free from its roots and dries out to a light, tangled ball of branches. This tumbles around in the wind, scattering **seeds** as it goes.

Steppe

'Steppe' is a Russian word that means 'vast, treeless' plain and we find such areas across North America and in Central Asia. Areas of steppe get less rain than prairies, but more than deserts. Mostly short grasses and **shrubs** grow here and plants do not grow as thickly as they do in the prairie.

Why are grasses so successful?

Grasses are tough plants. Burn them and they grow again, mow them down or set animals to graze on them and their leafy blades quickly reappear. Most plants grow from the tips of their **stems** and leaves, so can be damaged easily. Grass leaves grow from their base, close to the ground, so it does not matter if their tips are burnt, mown or nibbled.

There are several reasons why grasses can survive in drier parts of the world. Most grass leaves are curled up along their length. Rolled leaves reduce the amount of leaf space open to the weather and so reduce the amount of water lost as **water vapour** through the leaves. Also, most grass plants grow shallow **roots**, which spread far and wide in search of water and **nutrients**. As their many-branched roots decay, dead grasses add nutrients to the soil. This enriches the soil for the next generation of grass plants.

▲ Pampas is the name for the grasslands in Argentina and Uruguay. Pampas grass (*Cortaderia*) grows in tough clumps that root firmly into the poor soil. Its 2-m long stems hold up flowers from which thousands of seeds are blown for miles around.

Savannah

If you have ever watched TV programmes about African wildlife, you will have seen giraffes, wildebeest and lions living on hot, dry plains. The dusty ground is mostly covered with grass but also patches of trees and **shrubs**. This type of **habitat** is found not only in Africa but also in parts of Asia and Australia. It is called savannah.

Savannah grasses

Most savannah grasses grow in clumps or patches. On the driest patches of savannah, grasses may be short, but in moister places grasses can grow up to 4 metres tall. Savannah grasses do most of their growing during the rainy season. In the long and dusty dry season, most turn brown and growth is limited. They store moisture and **nutrients** in their **roots** while they await the return of the rainy season. After the rains, the savannah transforms into a green scene again. Grasses shoot up, flowers emerge from underground **bulbs** and **seeds**, and flushes of new leaves appear on trees.

Grass, grazers and predators

In savannah habitats like this one in Kenya, Africa, grasses provide food for vast herds of grazing zebra, antelope and wildebeest (pictured). **Predators** such as lions, cheetahs and hyenas hunt the grazing animals, using the grass to hide in.

Protect and survive

Clumps of larger trees such as palms grow in the moist soil near waterholes. However, other trees can only grow in this hot, dry habitat because they have **adapted** special ways of surviving. Some euphorbia and acacia trees store water in their tough **stems** and have small, leathery leaves to reduce the amount of water they lose by **evaporation**. In the wet season the baobab tree (*Adansonia digitata*) soaks up tonnes of water with its far-reaching roots, and stores it in its immense trunk.

The other big problem for savannah plants is grazing animals. Many seedlings are eaten by animals before they can grow into bushes or trees. As a defence, euphorbias have nasty-tasting, milky **sap**. Many acacia bushes and trees are covered with large thorns, but these do not put off all animals – many acacia trees have a flat-topped shape because of hungry giraffes. The branches can spread out only above the height of the tallest giraffes because those below get nibbled!

Ants and acacias

Some acacia trees are left well alone by grazers. The thorns of the whistling-thorn acacia (*Acacia drepanolobium*) are hollowed out and occupied by stinging ants. The ants stream out if a hungry mouth disturbs their home. Holes in old thorns, which the ants have vacated, whistle in the wind.

Scrubland

From a distance, scrubland looks as if a giant has scoured away a lot of the plant life. On closer inspection you find patches of slow-growing **shrubs** and small, stunted trees. Areas of scrubland are usually found on sandy soils near sea coasts, in places with hot, dry summers and mild, wet winters.

Kinds of scrub plants

Most scrub plants are **evergreens** with small, leathery leaves or needles. Their leaves are often full of **oils** that help stop water loss but also put off animals that want to eat them. Some of these oils give scrub plants, such as rosemary (*Rosmarinus*) and lavender (*Lavendula*), their characteristic smells. **Seeds** of **annual** plants lie **dormant** (resting) underground during the hot, dry summer. They **germinate** in winter after the rains. The plants that emerge from these seeds grow, flower and make their own seeds quickly, before the dry season returns.

▲ In this picture of a patch of scrubland in Portugal you can see some characteristic scrubland plants including lavender, broom (*Cistus*) and pines.

Scrubland around the world

Around the Mediterranean Sea scrubland is often called **maquis**. Maquis vegetation includes caper, rosemary and thyme bushes, and fig, bay, lemon and olive trees. In North American scrubland – called chaparral – there are flowering annuals such as tree poppies (*Dendromecon*) and forget-me-nots (*Myosotis*), and **perennials** such as sages, prickly pear (*Opuntia*) and scrub oak (*Quercus ilicifolia*). The world's largest scrublands are found in Australia – and are known as the bush. These very dry scrublands are rich in plant life, such as eucalyptus, flowering pea, myrtle and acacia trees.

Life-giving fires

During the dry season fires are common on scrubland. Although we think of fires as destructive, scrubland fires actually help to maintain plant life. Oils in some plants actually help fires to burn. Many scrub plants grow from wide **roots** close to the ground and grow back healthily within a year or so of burning. Fires also give the seeds of some flowering plants a chance to germinate in spaces where dense vegetation, which blocked the light, is burnt away.

▶ Banksias (*Banksia attenuata*) are evergreen bushes that grow in the Australian scrub. Their seed cases stay tightly closed for years, until fire sweeps through the bush and they open up in the heat. The seeds fall onto ground that is ideal for growth – cleared of other plants and made fertile by the ash of plants devoured by the flames.

Mountains

The higher that people climbing up a mountain go, the more problems they face. As they climb, they are more exposed to cold, wind and rain – even mountains in hot countries can have snow at the top – so they have to be equipped to protect themselves. Plants can grow only at particular levels of mountains because of the **climate** there. The different climate levels are called zones, and each zone supports a particular group of plants.

Plant zones

In the lowest zone of the Alps and many other mountain ranges, there are often **deciduous** trees, like birch and oak. Higher up the mountains, a zone of mostly **coniferous** trees, such as pine and fir, takes over. Higher still, the trees become smaller and more spaced out up to the tree-line – the level beyond which trees cannot grow because it is too cold. Above the tree-line only **shrubs** and other low-growing plants can thrive. These include tough flowering plants such as mountain avens (*Dryas octopetala*) and edelweiss (*Leontopodium alpina*), which grow close to the ground, out of the path of chill winds. The next zone up is a bare and rocky area where only the toughest plants, such as **mosses**, can survive. At the very top there may only be snow, ice and rock, and no plants at all.

◄ **If you look carefully at this picture you should be able to see different zones of plants. At the bottom, forests have been cleared for farming, but trees grow higher up until the tree-line.**

Mountain zones of the world

The plants that exist in the zones of individual mountain ranges may vary, but all mountains have different zones of plant life. In the Himalayas, the biggest mountain range in the world, the lowest zones have **tropical** plants, such as figs and palm trees and the middle zone supports many rhododendrons and bamboos.

On the hot and dry lower zone of Mount Kenya, on the **Equator** in Africa, there are grasses and scattered trees. The higher slopes have more rain than the ground, allowing trees such as cedar and tall bamboo plants to thrive. At even higher levels, plants face freezing temperatures at night and baking sun by day, with very little rain. Many tough grasses and other small plants can survive, but there are also big plants that have adapted to life at these rocky heights. Some survive the cold by making chemicals in their leaves that stop the water inside them freezing, while others protect their tender **buds** from the sun in pools of slime.

The giant groundsel

Around 4000 metres up Mount Kenya there are huge groundsel plants (*Senecio*), some of which look rather like giant cabbages. During the day, their thick leaves open up like the petals of a flower. They have a **waxy** surface and fleshy innards to stop them drying out in the sun. At night, when temperatures plummet, the leaves fold in, wrapping the more fragile central leaves in a protective embrace.

Ponds and lakes

The fresh water in ponds and lakes all over the world makes up only a tiny fraction of the Earth's total water, but forms a rich **habitat** for a huge variety of plants.

▲ The plants in a pond or lake provide shelter and food for many insects and animals. They also release oxygen into the water during photosynthesis, which helps to keep the water healthy.

Most freshwater plants have a ready supply of everything they need. Water is all around them, and although there is less **oxygen** and **carbon dioxide** in water than in air, there is plenty for them to carry out **photosynthesis**. **Nutrients**, from dead plant and animal matter and from the mud at the bottom of the pond, are dissolved in the water.

The only real problem freshwater plants have is a shortage of light – the deeper you go, the less light there is. Plants have different ways of ensuring they get enough light, depending on where in the pond or lake they live. Most grow by the edge, forming a fringe of green where water meets land. Plants, such as irises (*Iris*), sedges (*Carex*) and cattails (*Typha*), have their **roots** in the soil at the edge. While part of their stiff **stem** is under water, most hold their leaves and flowers up into the light.

The amazing Amazon Water lily

The leaves of the Amazon Water lily (*Victoria amazonica*) can be almost 2 metres across – big enough for an adult man to lie in (but not strong enough to support him). A single plant can grow about 50 of these leaves, which have air spaces within them that act like armbands to keep them afloat. On the underside of each leaf are ribs, like spokes in a wheel, that support the huge leaves.

Across shallow ponds or by the shores of deeper lakes some plants grow in slightly deeper water. These submerged plants still have their roots in the mud, but they have long stems that hold their leaves up to the light. To stay afloat at the surface, water lilies have flat and rounded leaves. They also have a **waxy** surface that repels rainwater and are shaped so the water runs off them – if too much water gathered on their leafy rafts, they would sink.

Not all water plants have their roots in the soil. In open water in the centre of a lake or pond, there are floating plants, such as duckweed (*Lemnaceae*) and water hyacinth (*Eichhornia crassipes*). Their tiny, hair-like roots dangle below the surface to collect water and dissolved nutrients. Duckweed plants have two tiny, leaf-like parts that are fleshy and filled with air to help them float. They grow together to form green mats in the centre of ponds.

Rivers and streams

Many of the plants in rivers and streams are similar to pond and lake plants, but they have an added challenge – the movement of the water makes it hard for them to stay upright or in one place, and their fragile parts can easily become damaged.

In fast-moving parts of a river, few plants survive, except for a few green **algae**, which make their homes growing flat on stones on the riverbed. Some plants manage to put down **roots** in calmer spots between rocks, and more find safe places to anchor roots in areas where the current slows down.

Leaves can easily be broken or damaged by moving water, so river plants have leaves that are able to cope with this problem. Some plants, such as eel grass (*Vallisneria*), have long thin leaves that offer little resistance to water flow. This means that they tend to drift in the direction of the water rather than trying to stand upright and fight against its flow. Others, such as water milfoil (*Myriophyllum spicatum*), have finely divided feathery leaves for the same reason. The water filters through them as it passes, rather than crashing against them.

◄ **Water crowsfoot or the yellow water buttercup (*Ranunculus fluitans*) has two different kinds of leaves. Its underwater leaves are fine and feathery to reduce water resistance and its surface leaves are rounded so they can float.**

Life on the edge

Many trees and other plants grow along the edge of rivers and streams. Ferns and **mosses** need damp conditions and cling to rocks next to streams, where they get splashed lightly with water as it passes. Trees such as alder (*Alnus*) and willow (*Salix*) also thrive in the damp soils by waterways. When alder **seeds** drop from their branches into the running water, they can travel long distances before being washed up onto a muddy shore. The seeds may then **germinate** in a new environment even more successfully than the seeds of their parent plant.

Plants on the edge have an important part to play in the health of the riverbank. Their roots bind the soil at the edge together, preventing the rushing water from washing it away (**erosion**). This is also important to the animal life in the river, because many creatures, including water voles and otters, make their burrows in the banks along waterways.

Waterfall plants

When river water rushes over a cliff, it crashes into a pool below and a cool mist is produced. The Angel Falls in Venezuela is nearly 1 kilometre high and thousands of tonnes of water pour over it each hour. Many plants thrive in the vast 'cloud forest' at its base. Every surface from cliff wall to tree branch is covered with **bromeliads**, orchids, mosses and ferns.

Swamps and marshes

Swamps and marshes are flat areas of waterlogged land, where water reaches or covers the surface of the ground for most of the time. Swamps often form where a lake has filled up with mud and plants, while marshes are common at the mouths of rivers where some water moves. Swamps and marshes both contain grasses such as cattails (*Typha*), bulrush (*Scirpus*) and sedges (*Cyperus*), but swamps have more trees than marshes, such as red maple (*Acer rubrum*), cypress (*Cupressus*) and alder (*Alnus*).

There are many grasses growing in wetland areas, from the giant papyrus (*Cyperus papyrus*) to the triangular **stemmed** sedges. They use extensive **root** networks to anchor themselves in the soggy ground. Soil and **sediment** gather around the roots, allowing other plants to establish themselves. **Rhizomes** spread rapidly through the sludge. New plants emerge from these underground stems, colonizing (taking over) large areas of land.

▶ Swamp cypresses (*Taxodium distichum*) are large **conifers** that live in swamps. Some of their roots grow upwards out of the water in the shape of traffic cones. These roots trap sediment from the water, making a supportive island of soil around each tree.

Insect-eating plants

In swamps and marshes, dead plants decay so slowly that the soil has a limited supply of **nutrients**. **Carnivorous** plants make food by **photosynthesis** as other plants do, but because the soil is poor they get the other nutrients they need from animals. Marsh pitchers (*Heliamphora*) have jug-shaped leaves containing digestive juices. Insects are attracted to the smell inside the pitcher but once they fall in the liquid, they cannot climb out again as the sides are too slippery. Bladderworts (*Utricularia*) live under water and suck in tiny animals through special trap doors.

Oxygen alert!

A major problem facing plants in swamps and marshes is that there is very little **oxygen** in the mud. Plants need oxygen for **respiration** (to release **energy** from their food) and they usually take it in through their roots. Marsh plants such as the cattail solve this problem by taking in air through their leaves and stems. They transport it to their roots through hollow tubes. Such plants often feel spongy, because of the large air-filled spaces inside them.

▼ Reeds and the giant papyrus dominate the swamps of the Okavango delta, Botswana.

Coastal wetlands

The muddy areas where rivers meet the sea make unique **habitats**. Plants here are gently soaked with fresh river-water for some of the time, then flooded with salty seawater when the **tides** come in. These twice-daily changes create a challenging environment.

▲ Some plants, such as salt marsh cordgrass (*Spartina alterniflora*), deal with the salt problem in another way. They take seawater up into their leaves and dispose of the salt through tiny holes called **stomata**.

Salty solutions

Seawater is harmful to most plants. In salt marshes and estuaries, many plants take in fresh water when they can and store it in fleshy **stems** or leaves. The common glasswort plant (*Salicornia europaea*) does just this – it looks rather like a tiny, shiny cactus, with its bright green, fleshy stems. Salt in seawater tries to soak up any fresh water in a plant. The leathery coating around leaves and stems on plants like samphire (*Crithmum Maritimum*) helps to prevent this.

Save the wetlands!

Many kinds of wetlands, including coastal marshes, have been drained and filled for farming or building. This is bad for wetland wildlife and for us. Wetlands are great floodbusters – soaking up water to stop it flooding land behind. They also act like giant sieves, catching mud that would **pollute** fresh water inland. **Conservation** agencies are now working hard to protect the world's wetlands.

Magical mangroves

Some muddy **tropical** shores are fringed with mangrove trees (*Rhizophora*), specially **adapted** to live in seashore mud. Most mangrove **roots** grow from halfway up the trunk, arching over like fingers poised to play a piano. They burrow down into mud a short distance from the main trunk. The knuckles of these finger-like roots stay above the water when the tide is in, gathering **oxygen** through special pores to supply to waterlogged roots below. Many root ends curl up into the air to collect oxygen too, making some patches of mud look like a bed of nails!

▲ This is the bright green root of a mangrove seedling, growing down from its parent tree.

The mangrove's grasping roots also help to anchor it in the moving surface of the mud. To give mangrove **seeds** a head start in this tricky environment, they **germinate** on the parent tree. Seedlings stay attached to the parent while they grow a long green spike root, which dangles in the air. When the spike is about 50 centimetres long, it falls off. If it is lucky enough to drop when the tide is out, it stands up in the mud. Within hours, tiny rootlets have sprung from it, enabling the young mangrove plant to get a firm enough grip on the mud to survive the incoming tide.

In the sea

When astronauts in space look back at Earth, the planet looks like a blue ball because oceans and seas cover almost three-quarters of its surface. Every continent and island of the world is fringed with coastlines, places where these waters meet the land.

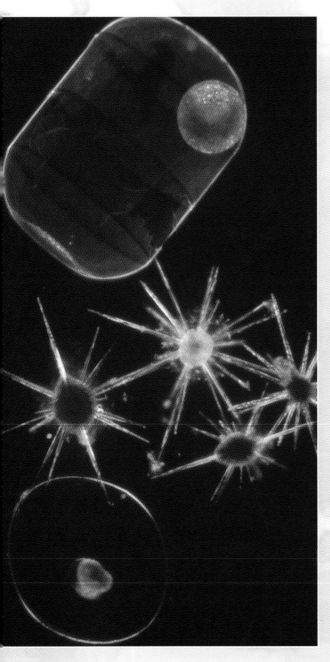

◄ This magnified picture shows tiny ocean algae, called diatoms. Their flattened shapes help them to stay afloat on the surface of the oceans.

Ocean algae

Very few plants live in deep seas, because plants need light for **photosynthesis** and light cannot reach down into deep water. However, tiny **algae** – plants without leaves, **stems**, **roots** or flowers – float on the waves, even far out to sea. Algae can be found all over the oceans, but large 'blooms' of algae are found in colder waters. Where the surface water is cold, deeper water rises, bringing with it essential **minerals**, such as iron, on which the algae flourish.

Ocean algae are known as phytoplankton. Just as on land, where plants are the source of all food for humans and other animals, algae are the basic food for all life at sea. Algae are also important for making **oxygen**, not only for animals at sea, but for the rest of us as well.

Shore life

Nearer the coastlines of the world, you find larger algae, called seaweed. Different kinds of seaweed grow at different places on the shore. Some, such as giant kelp (*Macrocystis pyrifera*), need to be covered in water all the time. They grow away from the shore in deepish water – some plants reach 60 metres in length – held tightly to the seabed with **holdfasts**.

Holdfasts look like roots but their job is just to hold the plants onto the rocks. Seaweed absorbs the water and **nutrients** it needs from the seawater around it through leaf-like **fronds**.

Seaweeds such as bladderwrack (*Fucus vesiculosus*), that grow at the edge of the shore, are under water when the **tide** is in and exposed to the weather when the tide is out. Many have fronds that float near surface water to catch the light when the tide comes in. When the water goes out, a coating of slime stops winds and sun from drying them out.

Sargasso Sea

There is an area of floating brown seaweed in the Atlantic Ocean thousands of square kilometres across. It is called the Sargasso Sea. It is held in place by slow currents and is so big it can be seen on satellite maps of the ocean. Millions of tiny marine animals live in it.

◄ The swollen bladders on seaweed like this are filled with air, which helps fronds to float.

By the seashore

Plants living on the seashore may not have to survive being immersed in water as seaweed does, but they do have to cope with burning sunshine, strong winds howling in from the sea, and salty spray blown in off the waves.

Rocky shores

The first colonizers of bare rock are **lichens**. As they die and crumble they can form a type of soil along with crumbling rock in clefts and ledges. Tough **mosses** but also flowering plants, such as the pink-flowering thrift (*Armeria maritima*) and round-leafed pennywort (*Hydrocotyle vulgaris*), can grow on this soil.

You rarely see trees on clifftops because it is too cold and windy for most, although some, such as blackthorn (*Prunus spinosa*) grow as dwarf (smaller) plants. Smaller plants, such as thistle, gorse (*Ulex europaeus*) and heather (*Calluna vulgaris*), grow amongst the tough grasses on top of cliffs.

Shingle beaches

Shingle beaches offer another challenge. Near the sea, shingle pebbles grind together as they are moved by the waves, making it almost impossible for plants to take root. Most can only survive at the top of the beach. Sea holly (*Eryngium maritimum*) grows on shingle banks. It has deep **roots** to take hold in the shingle and a strong **stem** that is not easily snapped by the wind.

▶ **The yellow-horned poppy (*Glaucium flavum*) is one of the deep-rooted flowering plants that can take hold in shingle.**

Dune-builders

Sand dunes are notoriously difficult for plants to grow in. Although some hot desert **species,** such as prickly pear and agave, can live on warm dunes, many cannot. Strong, salty winds from the sea blast across the beach and blow sand from one part of the dune to another, making it almost impossible for a plant to establish itself. However, several kinds of grass, such as marram grass (*Ammophila arenaria*) and sea oats (*Uniola paniculata*), thrive on dunes.

These grasses grow quickly and spread their long roots just under the surface of the sand, forming a tangled network that holds the sand in place. They also grow special underground stems called **rhizomes**, which stretch out beneath the surface and from which new plants can grow.

By catching the shifting sands so that they pile up around its roots, these important grasses also help other plants. As leaves and roots die, they form a rich layer of **humus** that mixes with the sand to make sandy soil. **Seeds** of other plants that blow onto the dune are then able to **germinate** in this soil. Dune-builders also prevent the beaches we enjoy visiting from being blown away and provide cover for many dune-living animals.

▼ A sand dune may look as if it is covered in hundreds of individual marram plants, but the many roots and rhizomes may be connected to a single plant!

Isolated islands

If you look closely at the oceans on a map of the world you will see many small islands dotted across them – often far from other lands – like freckles on the blue face of the sea.

▲ Tropical island beaches are often lined with palm trees that have grown from coconuts that washed ashore from the sea.

Invaders

Plants arrive on new, bare islands in many different ways. Many **seeds** travel by chance over short distances on floating bits of trees, which act as rafts. The seeds of a few **tropical** species, such as coconut (*Cocos nucifera*) and sea bean (*Entada gigas*), can survive for many months in the salt water and float over thousands of miles – but most will travel much shorter distances. When they wash up onto a beach with the right growing conditions, they may **germinate**.

Light seeds and spores of plants like grasses and ferns can be blown by the wind. Sticky seeds may be carried on a bird's or bat's feet. Or these flying animals may eat fruits on the mainland and release the seeds in droppings when they visit an island. Sometimes plants invade because of people. In the past, settlers of islands often brought familiar food plants with them to grow. These plants then started to grow wild.

Unique island plants

Many tropical islands have their own unique plant **species** that do not grow anywhere else in the world. Some of these plants have remained on their island **habitat** for millions of years. Sadly, when people arrived in the past to live on new islands, they often cut down plants to make room for villages. They also brought animals for meat or milk or as pets. The animals ate the plants but also disturbed other animals that **pollinate** the plants. Following these changes in island life, many of these amazing plants are now very rare.

Socotra – island of bizarre plants

Over one-third of the plant species on the island of Socotra, off north-east Africa, exist only there and they include some of the most bizarre plants in the world. When you scratch the **bark** of the dragon tree (*Dracaena cinnabari*) red **sap** seeps out, which reminded the people who named it of legendary dragon's blood. The red sap was once an important ingredient in different dyes and inks, and for varnishing (coating) violins. Another weird plant is a member of the cucumber family – the only one in the world to grow into a cucumber tree (*Dendrosicyos*). To survive droughts it keeps water stored in its thick trunk and sheds all its leaves.

▼ Leaves of the Socotra cucumber tree.

People and plants

As well as the many different natural **habitats** in the world, plants also live alongside people. Many of the plants that seem so familiar to us in our fields, parks and gardens are really a long way from their original home.

In the past, travellers brought back plant specimens from far and wide. They brought back some because they were beautiful to look at and others because they were good to eat. Carrots originally came from Afghanistan, tomatoes from Mexico and cauliflower from the Middle East. Brightly coloured rhododendrons once only grew in South-east Asia. Fuchsias came from Central and South America and New Zealand, and dahlias came from Mexico. Many popular house plants, such as philodendrons and ferns, are developed from **species** that live naturally in the shady floor of the rainforest.

Out of Africa

The African violet (*Saintpaulia*) was discovered in its natural habitat in Tanzania in 1892. Today it is a very popular houseplant in Europe and North America, because it thrives in warm homes and can flower all year round. Sadly it is now one of the rarest wild plants – there are few left in Tanzania as the forests where it lives are being destroyed.

▶ These citrus trees normally grow in the Mediterranean, but survive in a cooler place because they live in a warmed building, called an orangery, over winter.

◄ In some places where people have cleared ground and since abandoned it, plants are reclaiming the land. Yet, many of the plant species that have been lost by land clearance are now **extinct** and will never grow again.

Plant habitats in peril

Plants, then, have managed to find ways of growing on almost every part of the planet. They can survive for hundreds of years in deserts too hot for people and other animals to do much more than pass through. They can take root in places so cold most other living things would freeze to death within hours. There are plants that can survive salty seas, gale-force winds, drought or fire. The biggest threat to the plants on this planet does not come from their different and challenging environments – it comes from us!

People have been cutting down, burning and clearing large areas of trees and other plants to make way for buildings and farms for hundreds of years. Many people across the world are worried that this process of habitat destruction is speeding up. Rainforests are a prime example of this. They contain around half the world's plant species, but every second an area of rainforest trees the size of a football pitch is destroyed for timber or so the land can be used for grazing animals. Habitats like this take thousands of years to develop, and once destroyed, we may never see them again.

Try it yourself!

Try some of the activities on these pages to make some of your own plant **habitats** and to help protect some of the natural habitats across the world.

Create a mini-rainforest

You can make a very simple rainforest habitat using a plastic jar. It provides the warmth and keeps in the moisture that **tropical** plants need to grow.

You will need:

- A tall and wide clear plastic jar with lid (preferably recycled)
- A pair of gloves (rubber or gardening)
- Coarse gravel
- Activated charcoal powder
- Potting compost
- An old, long-handled wooden spoon
- Small tropical plants, such as a spider plant
- A water sprayer

Check your jar is clean inside. Then put the gloves on to protect your hands. Add handfuls of gravel to make a lower layer, then handfuls of compost mixed with a little charcoal to make an upper layer. Make holes for the plants using the spoon. Take them out of their pots and gently put the plants in the holes, firming the soil around the **roots** using the spoon. Spray lots of water on the plants and soil and put the lid on the pot. Put the jar in a light, fairly warm place and wait for your rainforest plants to establish themselves!

Design a desert!

Make your own desert, complete with cacti. Cacti need warmth but very little moisture to thrive. In fact, you only need to water them once every two to three months!

You will need:

- A flat terracotta pot
- A pair of gloves (rubber or gardening)
- Coarse gravel
- Activated charcoal powder
- Potting compost
- Sand
- Mixed cacti and stone plants
- Larger rocks for scenery

Follow the same procedure as for creating a rainforest. First put in the gravel, then a thin layer of charcoal and then a thicker layer of soil to within 2 centimetres of the top of the pot. Then put on the gloves (cacti can be quite prickly) and plant the cacti and stone plants so that their roots are only just under the soil surface. Add the larger rocks and finally a thin layer of sand to cover the compost between the plants. Water the soil until it is just damp. Set the pot on a sunny windowsill inside your home or school where it is out of the way.

Remember – those spines can hurt! Once you have found a place, try not to disturb the plants.

Grow your own air plant

Air plants (*Tillandsia*) don't need soil to grow. Their long, stiff leaves take in water and **nutrients** from the air. The leaves are more like roots, and the root's main job is to anchor the plant. Try growing your own.

You will need:

- An air plant. (Ask your local garden centre for advice on what to choose from what is available near you.)
- A piece of driftwood or old wood
- Wire
- Sphagnum moss or Spanish moss
- A water mist sprayer
- Plant food (fertilizer)

Fasten your air plant to the piece of driftwood or old wood using the wire. (Make sure you don't put the plant base in a hole in the wood as water could collect there and the plant might rot.) Use a little **moss** to hide the wire. Stand your wood in bright, indirect light if possible, and normal indoor temperatures are fine.

You should spray the air plant every day with a light mist of water. If you forget and your plant becomes very dry you can give it a thorough drenching in the sink or shower on occasion.

You should also give the plant a dose of plant food (fertilizer) once a month. Follow the instructions on the packet.

Looking at plant habitats

These lists give some of the plants you can find in habitats around the world.

Rainforest

Tall trees: fig (*Ficus*), teak (*Tectona grandis*), mahogany (*Swietenia macrophylla*), rosewood (*Aniba rosaeodora*), ebony (*Diospyros ebenum*), ironwood, eucalyptus and Brazil **nut** (*Bertholletia excelsa*)

Climbers and stranglers: rattans (climbing palms), lianas, yam (*Dioscorea*), sweet potato (*Ipomoea batatas*), cheese plant (*Monstera tenuis*)

Epiphytes: orchids (including vanilla orchid), ferns, **bromeliads**, even cacti

Shrubs and small trees: palms (banana, oil and rubber), avocado (*Persea americana*), cocoa, coffee, lychee, mango, nutmeg, breadfruit

Broad-leaved forest

Deciduous broad-leaved trees: oak (*Quercus*), cherry (*Prunus*), ash (*Fraxinus*), beech (*Fagus*), southern beech (*Nothofagus*), birch (*Betula*), hickory (*Carya*), maple (*Acer*), walnut (*Juglans*), elm (*Ulmus*), hazel, hornbeam, chestnut (*Castanea*), basswood (*Tilia*), sweetgum (*Liquidambar*)

Shrubs and smaller plants: dogwood (*Cornus*), cyclamen (*Cyclamen*), primrose (*Primula vulgaris*), ivies, violet (*Viola*), horsetail, bamboo, wood anemone (*Anemone nemorosa*)

Climbers: poison ivy (*Rhus radicans*), virginia creeper (*Parthenocissus quinquefolia*), honeysuckle (*Lonicera*)

Epiphytes: ferns, mosses, clubmosses

Evergreen broad-leaved trees: magnolia (*Magnolia grandiflora*), camphor (*Cinnamomum camphora*), evergreen oak (*Quercus*), blackwood, eucalyptus (*Eucalyptus*), mulberry (*Morus*)

Coniferous forest

Coniferous trees: balsam firs (*Abies balsamea*), black spruces (*Picea*), jack pines (*Pinus banksiana*), white spruces (*Picea glauca*), redwoods and sequoias (*Sequoia*), douglas firs (*Pseudotsuga menziesii*), western hemlock, cypress (*Cupressus*), cedars (*Cedrus*), larch (*Larix*), monkey puzzle (*Araucaria*)

Hot desert

Succulents: saguaro (*Carnegia gigantea*), prickly pear (*Opuntia*), barrel cactus (*Ferocactus*), agaves (*Agave*), old man cactus (*Cephalocereus senilis*), aloes (*Aloe*)

Shrubs and smaller plants: creosote bush (*Larrea tridentata*), big sagebrush (*Artemisia tridentata*), prickly poppies (*Argemone*), yucca (*Yucca*), desert paintbrush (*Castilleja chromosa*), ocotillo (*Fouquieria splendens*), welwitschia plant

(*Welwitschia mirabilis*), euphorbias (*Euphorbia*), stone plants (*Lithops*)

Trees: palo verde trees (*Cercidium*), joshua tree (*Yucca brevifolia*), cottonwood tree (*Populus fremontii*), crucifixion palm (*Chaparro amargosa*), mesquite (*Prosopis*)

Scrubland

Trees: cork oak (*Quercus suber*), eucalyptus, karri, cedar (*Cedrus*), cypress (*Cupressus*), redwood (*Sequoia*), olive (*Olea*), lemon, manzanita (*Arbutus unedo*), scrub oak (*Quercus ilicifolia*), carob, cycads, Torrey pine (*Pinus torreyana*)

Shrubs: myrtle (*Myrtus communis*), oleander (*Nerium oleander)*, rosemary (Rosmarinus), lavender (*Lavendula*), sage (*Salvia*), oregano, chamise shrub (*Adenostoma*), thyme (*Thymus*), broom (*Cytisus*)

Succulents: agave (*Agave*), prickly pear (*Opuntia*), euphorbia (*Euphorbia*)

Smaller flowering plants: amaryllis, gladiolus

Grasslands

Grasses: canada wild rye (*Elymus canadensis*), pampas grass (*Cortaderia*), wheat, big bluestem (*Andropogon gerardii*), Indian grass (*Sorghastrum nutans*), prairie cord grass (*Spartina pectinata*), switch grass (*Panicum virgatum*), sideoats grama (*Bouteloua curtipendula*)

Other flowering plants: sagebrush (*Artemisia tridentata*), asters (*Aster*), prairie blazing star (*Liatris pycnostachya*), sweet coneflower (*Rudbeckia submentosa*), sunflower (*Helianthus*), prairie clover (*Petalostemum*), morning glory (*Ipomoea*), milkweed (*Asclepias*)

Trees and shrubs: willow (*Salix*), poplar (*Populus*), alder (*Alnus*), ombu tree (*Phytolacca dioica*)

Savannah

Grasses: fountain grass (*Pennisetum setaceum*), elephant grass (*Pennisetum purpureum*), bermuda grass (*Cynodon dactylon*)

Shrubs: sickle bush (*Dichrostachys cinerea*), velvet bushwillow (*Combretum molle*), mimosa (*Albizia*)

Trees: acacias, e.g. umbrella thorn (*Acacia tortilis*), sweet thorn (*Acacia karoo*), torchwood (*Balanites maughamii*), baobab (*Adansonia digitata*), candelabra tree (*Euphorbia ingens*), marula (*Sclerocarya birrea*), mimosa, palms (e.g. Senegal date palm), Cape chestnut (*Calodendrum capense*), cabbage tree (*Andira inermis*), kei apple (*Dovyalis caffra*)

Glossary

adapt/adaptation when a plant or animal gradually changes over thousands of years to fit in with an aspect of the habitat in which it lives or the special features that make it better able to survive and reproduce in its habitat

algae types of plant that do not have leaves, stems, roots or flowers. We call them plants because they can use sunlight to make their own food in the process of photosynthesis.

annual plant that grows, flowers, makes seeds and dies all within one year (or season)

bark outer skin of a tree

broad-leaved kind of tree with broad, flat leaves

bromeliad type of epiphyte (plant that grows on another plant for support) that collects rainwater in waxy leaves that form cups

bud swelling on a plant stem of tiny, young, overlapping leaves or petals and other parts of a flower, ready to burst into bloom

bulb underground bud protected by layers of thick, fleshy leaves. An onion is a kind of bulb.

canopy top layer of a forest, where the branches of the trees spread out to form a leafy roof

carbon dioxide gas in the air around us that plants use for photosynthesis

carnivorous describes a plant that digests parts of insects or other animals for food

chlorophyll green substance found in plants that is used in photosynthesis. Chlorophyll gives leaves their green colour.

climate general pattern of weather in an area over a period of years

cone form of dry fruit (in which seeds develop) produced by conifer trees. Cones are often egg-shaped and they are made up of lots of overlapping scales.

conifer kind of tree that has needle-like leaves and bears its seeds in cones

coniferous word used to describe a conifer tree

conservation type of work people do to protect the natural habitats of the world

corm swollen underground stem grown by some plants

deciduous describes plants that lose all their leaves in winter

dormant describes a plant during its resting period, which occurs particularly in winter. Seeds may lie dormant in winter when it is cold, and begin to grow in spring warmth.

energy ability in living things to do what they need to do in order to live and grow. Plants and animals get the energy they need from their food.

epiphyte plant that grows on another plant for support, often to get itself into a good position for receiving sunlight

Equator imaginary line around the centre of the Earth

erosion process by which water, wind, frost or rain break rock and soil loose from one area of land and move them to another

evaporates/evaporation when water turns from liquid into a vapour (a gas). When clothes dry on a line it is because the water evaporates and the vapour becomes part of the air.

evergreen describes plants that lose some old leaves and grow some new leaves all year round so they look green all the time

extinct when every individual plant of a species (kind) has died

fertile when soil is rich and healthy for plants to grow in

frond leaf-like part of plants such as ferns and seaweed

germinate when a seed starts to grow

habitat type of environment in which a plant or animal lives such as a mountain habitat or a rainforest habitat

holdfast root-like part of a seaweed. Holdfasts attach seaweed to the ground. They do not take in water and nutrients as real roots do.

humid hot and moist

humus crumbly kind of soil rich in dead plant matter

leaf litter when dead leaves fall to the ground they form a carpet of rotting plant matter called leaf litter. Fungi and many small animals live among and feed on leaf litter.

lichen plant formed by an alga and a fungus growing together. Most are small and tend to grow on walls, rocks and tree trunks.

liverwort simple plant that is closely related to mosses. Liverworts have no stems or leaves and look rather like small, flat seaweed.

maquis French word for chapparal, a kind of scrubland dominated by grasses and shrubs

minerals chemical building blocks of rocks. Plants need some minerals and elements (such as copper and calcium) in order to grow and reproduce.

moss tiny green plants that grow together in their hundreds in damp places, forming cushion shapes

nut kind of dry fruit. The hard shell of a nut is the fruit. The inner part, which we sometimes eat, is the seed.

nutrients kinds of chemicals which nourish plants and animals

oil greasy substance that does not dissolve in water

oxygen gas in the air that plants help supply by releasing it during the process of photosynthesis

parasite plant plant that lives on and gets its food from another living thing

perennial describes a plant that lives for more than two years, often for many years

photosynthesis process by which plants make their own food using water, air and energy from sunlight

Pole the North Pole and the South Pole are at opposite ends of the Earth. The Earth rotates on its axis and the Poles are where the axis comes out at the Earth's surface.

pollinate/pollination when pollen travels from the anthers of one flower to the stigma of the same or a different flower

pollute poison or harm any part of the environment (the natural world)

predator animal that preys on (catches and eats) another animal

reproduce when a living thing produces young like itself

respiration process by which living things release energy from their food

rhizome special kind of stem that grows under the ground instead of up in the air

root plant part that grows underground and takes in water and nutrients

sap fluid containing food made in the leaves. Sap flows in a plant's phloem tubes.

sediment particles (very tiny bits) of rock in water

seed the part of a plant that contains the beginnings of a new plant

shrub woody stemmed, tree-like plants that do not grow above 6 metres tall

species kind of living thing

stem part of the plant that holds it upright and supports its leaves and flowers

stomata tiny openings on a leaf, usually on the underside, which let water vapour and oxygen out and carbon dioxide in

succulent plant that has fleshy leaves or stem, where water is stored

temperate describes areas that have warm summers, cold winters and light rain throughout the year

tide rise and fall of the sea. At high tide the sea rises up the beach. At low tide it flows down again.

tropical found in the tropics – countries around the Equator which have some of the hottest climates in the world

tuber short, thick underground stem. New tubers (and from those, new plants) can grow from the buds (called 'eyes') on a tuber.

water vapour when water evaporates (turns from a liquid into a gas) it becomes water vapour. Water can evaporate from leaves when air temperature increases or when wind blows across a plant.

wax/waxy natural, plastic-like substance. Plants often have a very thin layer of wax around their leaves or fruits to stop them from drying out.

Find out more

Books

Eyewitness Guides: Plant and *Tree*, David Burnie, Dorling Kindersley

Eyewitness Visual Dictionaries: Plants, Deni Brown, 1992, Dorling Kindersley

Internet-linked Library of Science: World of Plants, L. Howell and K. Rogers, 2001, Usborne
www.usborne.com/quicklinks/quicklinks.asp

Magic School Bus: Plants and Seeds, Joanna Cole and Bob Degen, 1999, Econo-clad Books

Plants, Jo Ellen Moore, 1986, Evan-Moor Educational Publishers

The Oxford Children's Encyclopedia of Plants and Animals, 2000, Oxford University Press

The Private Life of Plants, David Attenborough, 1995, BBC Books; also available as a set of videos of the BBC television series of the same name.

Websites

Great Plant Escape: fun way of learning about what different plant parts do; also a simple glossary of terms
www.urbanext.uiuc.edu/gpe/gpe.html

BBCi nature: gardening calendar, fun facts and links to Private Life of Plants information based on TV series presented by Sir David Attenborough
www.bbc.co.uk/nature/plants/

Alien explorer: looks at what plants are like and where they grow, from an outsider's point of view!
www.alienexplorer.com/ecology/topic27.html

Blooming of the titan arum: a website devoted to one of the world's most remarkable flowers – you can see its bud opening!
www.news.wisc.edu/titanarum/index.html

Habitats of the world: at Missouri Botanical Garden's website, you can compare the habitats of the world
mbgnet.mobot.org/index.htm

Conservation sites

Information of dangers to wild plants and habitats and what conservation groups are doing to help them survive

Worldwide Fund for Nature
www.wwf.org.uk

Friends of the Earth
www.foe.co.uk/campaigns/biodiversity

Eden Project: lots of information about the remarkable Eden greenhouses, where different plant habitats have been created, plus an interesting plant quiz
www.edenproject.com

Places to visit

Many museums, arboretums (botanical garden devoted to trees) and botanic gardens are fascinating places to visit. You could try:

The Royal Botanical Gardens, Kew, near London

Westonbirt Arboretum, Gloucestershire

Eden Project, St Austell, Cornwall

You can also find out about plants by visiting local garden centres.

Index

Titles in the *Life of Plants* series include:

Hardback   0 431 11883 3

Hardback   0 431 11881 7

Hardback   0 431 11884 1

Hardback   0 431 11880 9

Hardback   0 431 11885 X

Hardback   0 431 11882 5

Find out about the other titles in this series on our website www.heinemann.co.uk/library